BOND ON SET

GREG WILLIAMS

007 FILMING DIE ANOTHER DAY

First published 2002 by Boxtree, an imprint of Pan Macmillan Ltd
Pan Macmillan, 20 New Wharf Road, London N1 9RR
Basingstoke and Oxford

www.panmacmillan.com

Associated companies throughout the world

ISBN 0 7522 6499 0 [PBK]
ISBN 0 7522 1561 2 [HBK]

James Bond™, 007™ and Die Another Day© 1962-2002
Danjaq, LLC and United Artists Corporation. All Rights Reserved

James Bond™, 007™ and Die Another Day are trademarks
of Danjaq, LLC, Licensed by EON Productions Limited

All photographs© 2002 Greg Williams
Edited by Emma Marriott and Natalie Jerome
Text© 2002 Eon Productions Limited. All Rights Reserved.
Except interviews with John Cleese, Vic Armstrong,
Rosamund Pike and Andrew Paul Smith© 2002 Greg Williams
Designed by Mike Bone, Bostock and Pollitt Ltd, London
Printed by Bath Press

9 8 7 6 5 4 3 2 1

A CIP catalogue record for this book is available from the
British Library

I got to know Greg Williams when I was on location with the Second Unit in Iceland. I had met Greg before, he had done a special shoot for us on *The World Is Not Enough*, but I did not have the chance to sit down and talk to him until Iceland. When you spend a week with someone on a frozen lake, five miles from land in a survival suit and crampons, you do get to know them. I had the opportunity to watch Greg work. We both were taking pictures. When we were about to film a stunt, I would place myself near one of the unit camera positions – the preferred position of professional 'stills' photographers around the world. Greg, on the other hand, would wander all around studying the location from every angle. Finally, he would pick his own spot, usually halfway up some iceberg. When filming stunts, professional stills men use several radio-controlled motor driven cameras in different positions in the hope of capturing the one definitive picture. Greg used one conventional camera that would fire only as fast as he could hand wind it. You don't have to guess who got the best pictures, they are in this book.

Greg is a big man and I used to wonder how he was going to be unobtrusive enough on a film set to get his signature candid shots. I think his secret is an endearing charm that disarms the hard-boiled movie pro and instantly soothes the high-strung artist. Greg manages to merge into the environment becoming part of the background while standing only a few feet from his subject. Only the barely perceptible click of his Leica reveals his presence.

Technical proficiency and a keen eye are just prerequisites for a reportage photographer. To instinctively know the defining moment and then to be in exactly the right place at the right time is what distinguishes a master. It was a pleasure to see a master at work.

INTRODUCTION
PIERCE BROSNAN

The great joy of these photos and this kind of book is that you get to pull back the curtain and immerse yourself in the art of filmmaking. Sometimes it's just a candid portrait of an actor before the director says 'action', other times, it's a tableau of actors, propmen, cameras and confusion that all comes together in a single image that enthrals and bemuses.

The culmination of Greg Williams and Bond in its twentieth anniversary is a marriage made in heaven. Never before have we seen backstage intimacies of a Bond movie in such a classic book as this. Greg captures the moment and processes all the senses into one image. I respect that he does this in an environment that is not always easy or welcoming.

I love looking at old photos of Hollywood as opposed to the plenitude of 'behind-the-scenes' TV shows, of which there are too many now-a-days. There is nothing like a black and white photo taken by a photographer who knows his craft, and who knows how to fit into the crazy world of a movie set, while finding the hidden moments before the action begins and the director says 'cut'.

I still get excited walking onto movie sets or even passing one in the street, whether it be London or Hollywood. They have an air of mystery, romance, glamour and just plain old hard work. From Greg's photos, you get to observe that particular moment in time just before the actor steps up to his mark.

The absurdity of standing there wet and cold, gripping a hot water bottle, waiting for the next take and all the time trying to hold on to your dignity while playing James Bond – not easy. But that's why the book is so cool. The moments of doubt and fear, not knowing if it will all come together, and then... the magic... the smiles of relief when the words and actions fall into place.

This book illustrates the work that we do, the fun that we have and the process of making *Die Another Day*. I hope it will be enjoyed by the legions of fans who love the Bond films and by all of us who love the movies.

Hats off to you Greg!

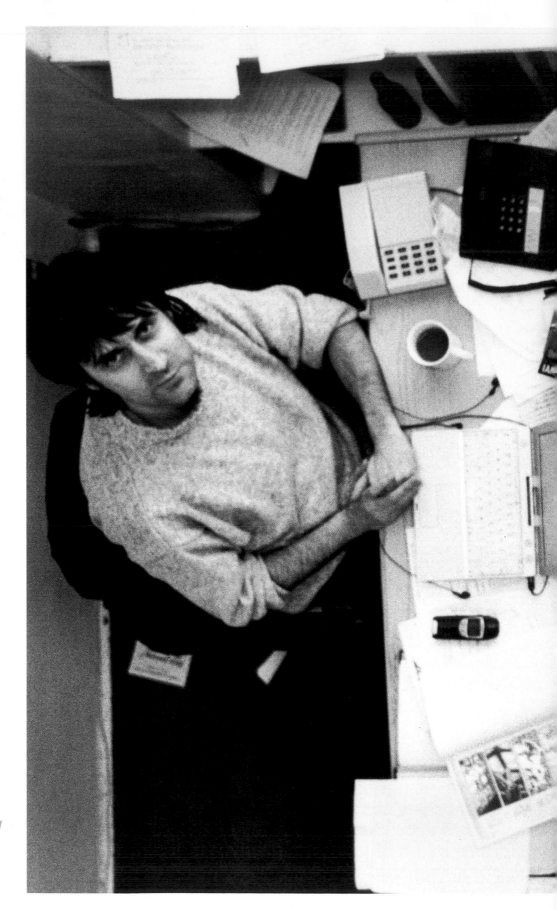

'People might think writing a Bond film is easy – you've got Bond, M, Q, Moneypenny, some beautiful girls and a villain. But that's what makes it actually quite daunting. How do you make it all seem fresh and new?'
Neal Purvis and Robert Wade, Writers

Above: Peter Lamont, Production
Designer on the back lot of Pinewood
Studios; exterior of the Ice Palace
Below: On the set of the North/South
Korean divide

015

Above: Stuntman Mark Mottran demonstrates
to Pierce Brosnan the correct procedure for
dealing with a henchman
Right: Colonel Moon played by Will Yun Lee

Previous page: 'I got injured, the old knee went. Well, it's a physical film and you're trying to put yourself in the action as much as possible. I was running away from all the Koreans, thinking I didn't need to stretch and pounded the old knee out.'
Pierce Brosnan, 007

The moment the decision was made to put the filming of *Die Another Day* in hiatus for seven filming days as Pierce Brosnan was flown to LA for an emergency operation on his knee

This page, clockwise from left: Barbara Broccoli, Anthony Waye, Michael G. Wilson, Callum McDougall, David Tattersall, Sasha Turjak and Lee Tamahori

Right: Director Lee Tamahori in Bond's
North Korean cell

Over page: 'They rang up and said they want
to call you for the Bond girl. I said "Great, you
know, why not?" And I went in and it was this
extraordinary process. You go in one day then
its instantly "The director wants to meet you",
then it's "We want to take you to Pinewood for
a screen test", then it's "Right we're sending
those tapes to America" then it's "Right you've
got the job." In eight days it's the most
extraordinary escalating change of life.'
Rosamund Pike, Miranda Frost, MI6 agent

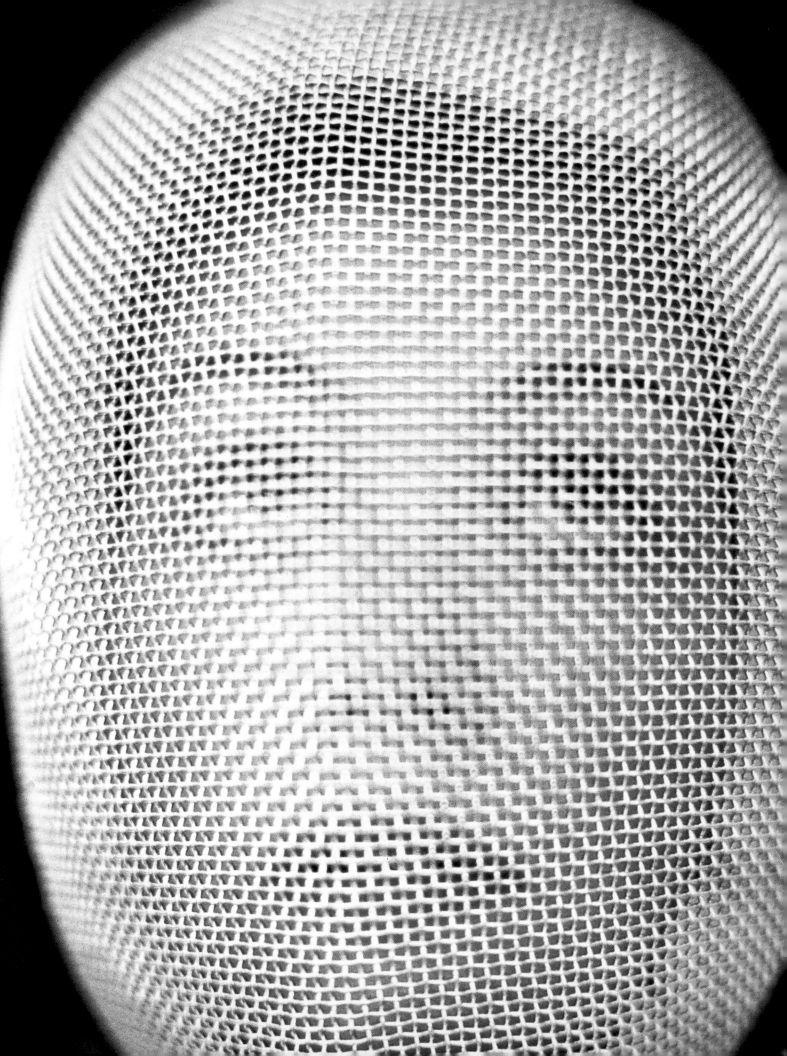

Bond's surfboard

Over page: Bond's transformation into captured prisoner. The prisoner exchange sequence takes place on a bridge at the North/South Korean border

'The James Bond character is so complex and multi-faceted that you can always tap into some new aspect. Particularly with Pierce, he has such great vulnerability and humanity which enables us to go into areas we haven't done before and give Bond some moral challenges.'
Barbara Broccoli, Producer

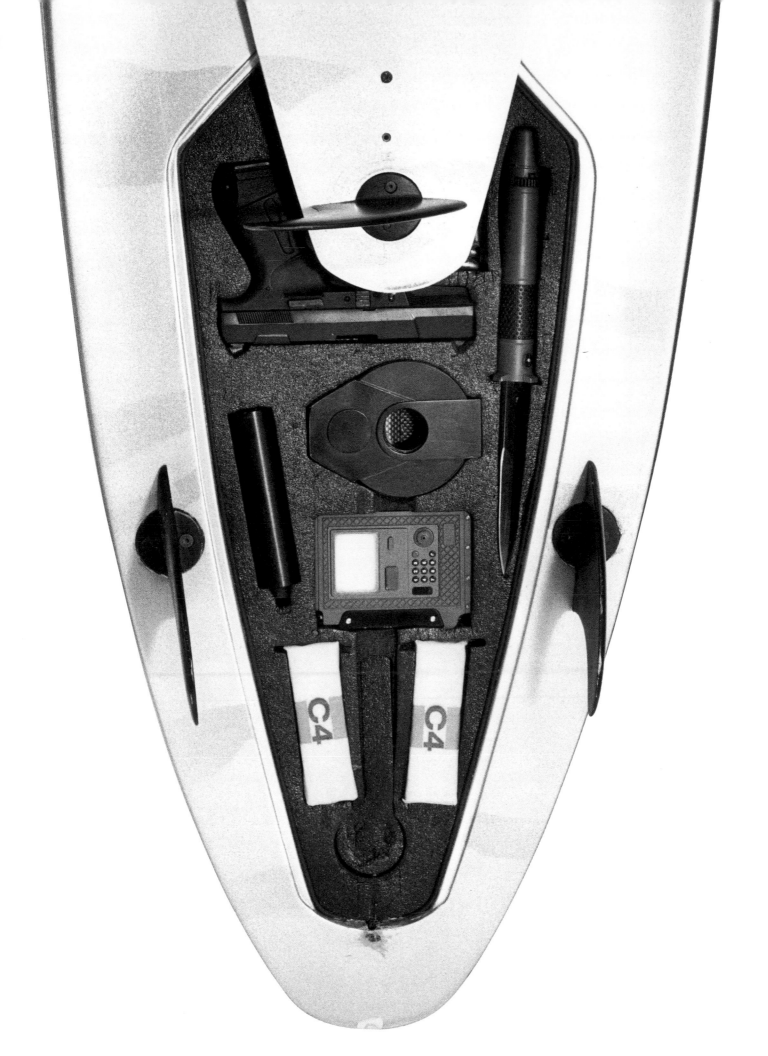

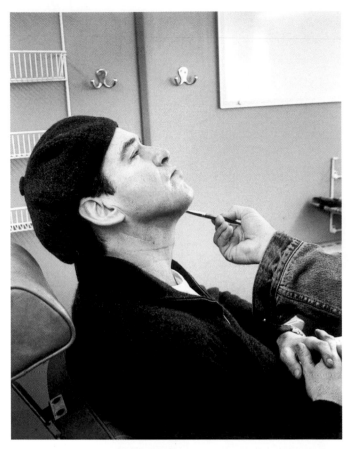

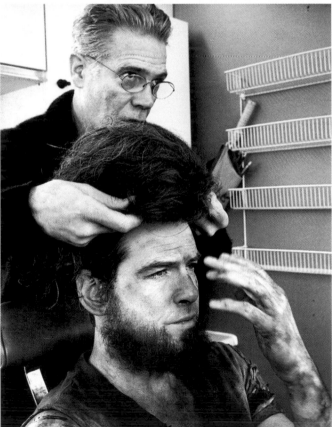

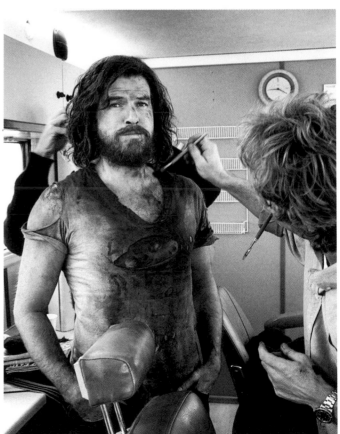

'When Lindy Hemming (Costume Designer)
was describing the cut of Bond's suit –
I wasn't quite sure what she was talking about.
But then I put it on and the suit really makes
you stand up straight. And you know he's a
Commander so you have that presence.'
Pierce Brosnan, 007

Over page: Filming the title sequence

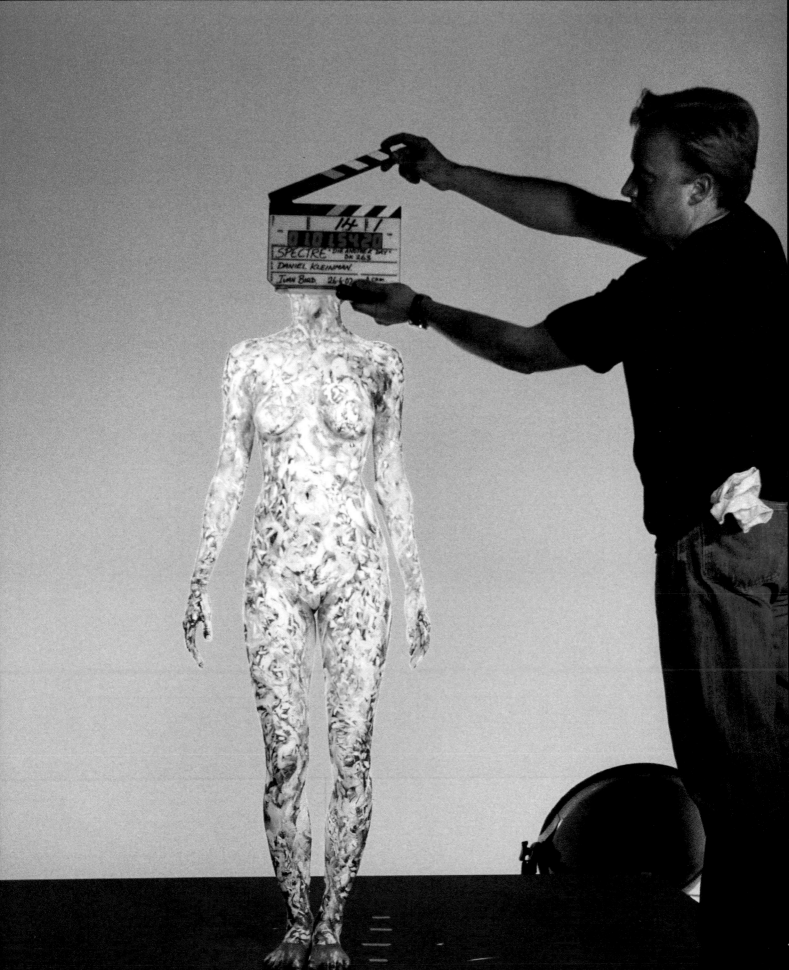

Right: Pierce Brosnan's make-up artist,
Bron Roylance, retouches him for scenes
filmed in the MI6 office

Above: Judi Dench talks through an action sequence with a stuntman

'I think M cares a great deal about Bond. Its not her job to show it, but she does and she knows he's the best.'
Judi Dench, M

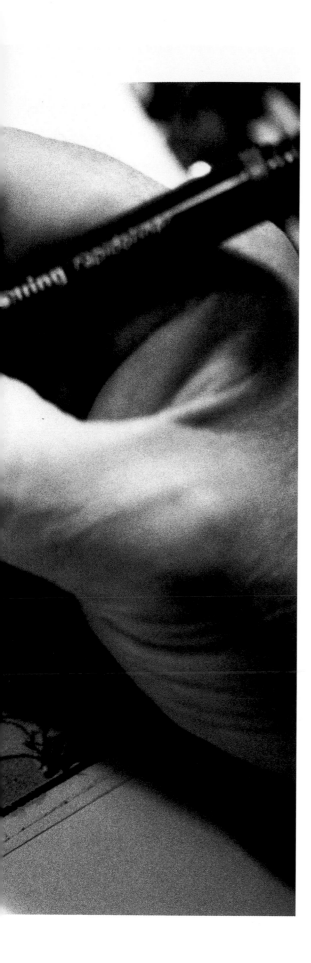

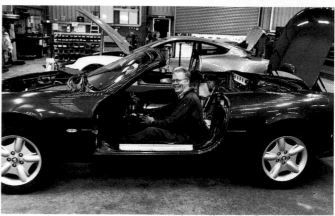

Above: A script meeting attended by the Writers, Producers and Director Lee Tamahori

Below: The Bond car workshop

Bond in the virtual reality
shooting range

'Q is someone who loves gadgets and is thoroughly irritated by Bond's lifestyle and wishes that he would treat the gadgets much better. If Bond got killed in the process then, you know, at least the gadgets would be all right.'
John Cleese, Q

Over page: 'I've been seeding all these little homages to past Bond movies without overpowering this one. Those who love Bond movies will see them all, there's probably going to be about fifteen to twenty of them all the way through the movie. I said, why don't we fill one of these rooms with all the gadgets from old Bond movies? Stuffed alligators, Rosa Klebb's shoe, the briefcase from *From Russia with Love*, they're everywhere, they're laid all over the place, there's the jetpack from *Thunderball*. And it was to be viewed as a kind of relic room, where all the gadgets were just thrown in the corner. We decided to play all the old paraphernalia, almost like a museum.'
Lee Tamahori, Director

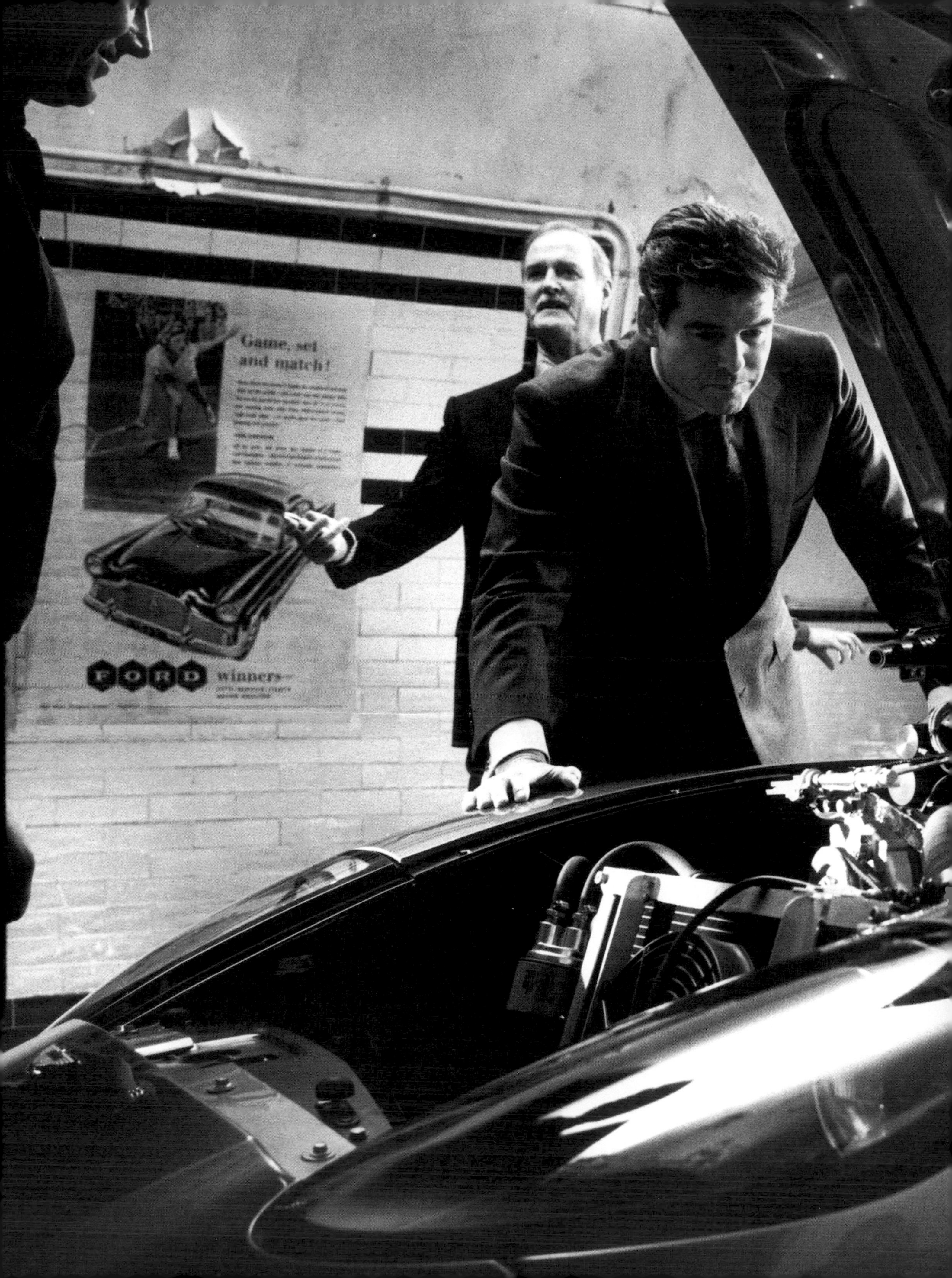
Game, set
and match!
FORD winners

Left: 'I play Gustav Graves who's essentially the [main] Bond villain. This scene is the entrance of my character into the film. He is parachuting into Buckingham Palace to be knighted. Graves's origins are unspecified but we think he was born in Argentina and considers Britain to be his adopted country. He's trying to be more British than the British.'
Toby Stephens, Gustav Graves

Above: Bond and Graves' stuntmen filming
on the set of Blades fencing club

'I grew up watching Bond and sort of fantasizing about being in that world of mystery and intrigue and all the gadgets and fun, so to have the chance to be part of it is just like sheer, sheer fun and joy.'
Halle Berry, Jinx

Above: Halle Berry with Anthony Waye, Executive Producer

The crew on set in Cadiz, Spain filming
Halle Berry emerging from the sea in
a scene reminiscent of *Dr No*

'Bond watches Jinx come out of the surf and she comes up, she sees him, he sees her and there's this kind of tease, but ultimately they both just want to go for it.'
Pierce Brosnan, 007

Over page: 'Jinx is very feisty and tough. Intellectually and physically she is in many ways a match for Bond and very in control of who she is, a woman on a mission, like he is.'
Halle Berry, Jinx

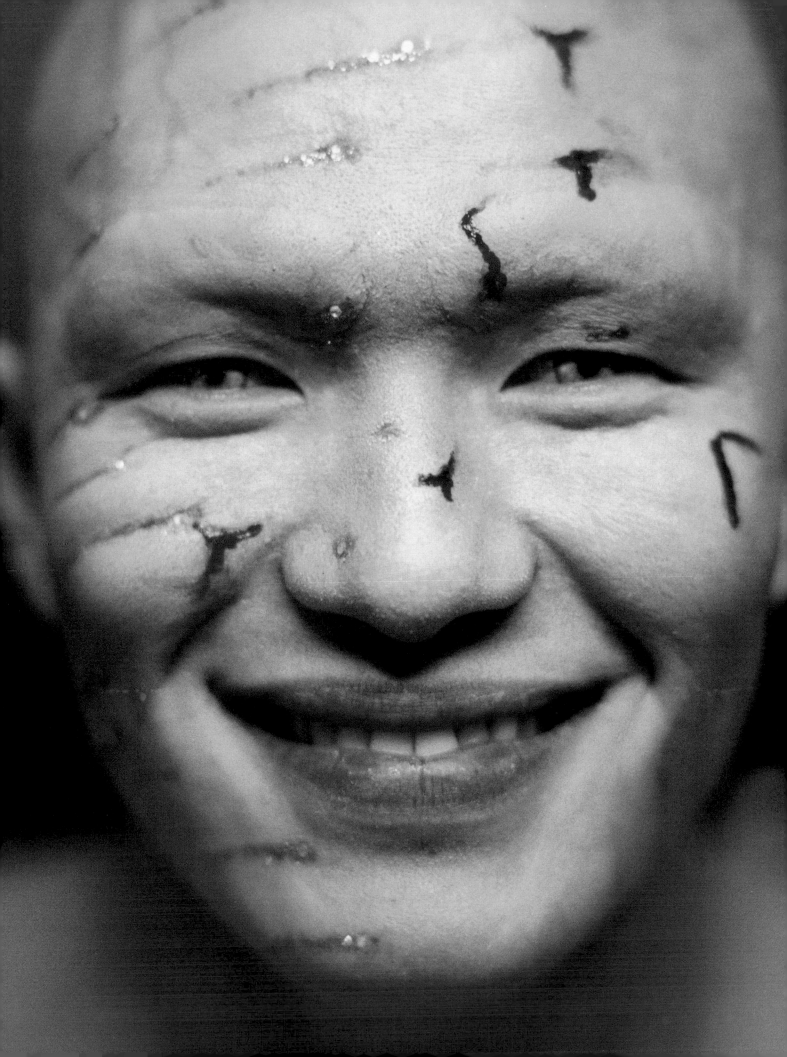

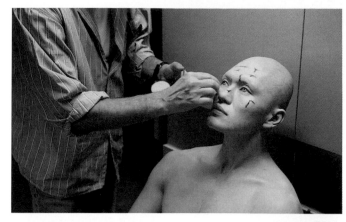

Left: 'The DNA change was something that
we had to come up with, a proper sort of
transformation. We tried to rebuild Rick Yune,
the actor who plays Zao, into something that
was halfway believeable and a bit more spirited
to make it a Bond villain. We embellished the
fact that he's blown up with diamonds and we
made them more of a tribal marking.'
Paul Engelen, Make-up Supervisor

Previous page: Director Lee Tamahori
with Raoul, Bond's Cuban contact, played by
Emilio Echevarria

Bond exits Dr Alvarez's clinic in Cuba

Over page: Michael Madsen plays Falco,
the agent working alongside Jinx from
the American National Security Agency

Left: Deleted scene from *Die Another Day*. Jinx has just killed Dr Alvarez (played by Simon Andreu) at his clinic in Cuba, and is stealing a CD containing Zao's gene therapy programme

Above: The day Halle Berry found out she had been nominated for an Academy Award

Over page: Joking around between takes in a scene in the bunker. L-r, Michael G. Wilson, Michael Madsen, Judi Dench and Colin Salmon

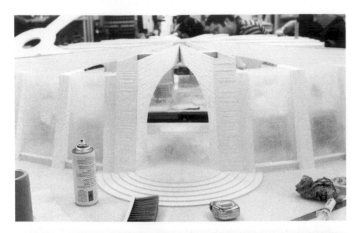

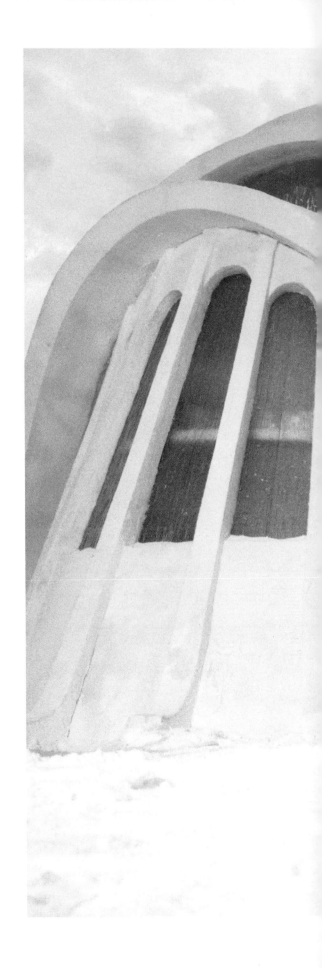

Creating the Ice Palace. From initial design as a model, to full-scale section in a studio at Pinewood. Finally the scale model on the back lot

'Rosamund is extraordinarily keen and eager and looks fantastic. She's got a lot of old-fashioned movie-star qualities I've noticed, quite rare these days. I'm not sure what that is, but there's an elegance to her, the way she holds herself. Very Hepburnesque.'
Lee Tamahori, Director

Over page: Halle Berry wearing the fuchsia crystal dress, designed by Donatella Versace. Costume Designer Lindy Hemming saw a similar Versace dress in a fashion magazine and requested Donatella to make one to her specifications

Gene therapy has a side effect – permanent insomnia. 'One hour a day on the dream machine keeps me sane.' Graves to Zao

Above: 'Originally the ice dragster started off as an ice yacht. We adapted the body, added a couple of jets, a propulsion unit and modified the front skis. On the frozen lake it looks stunning.'
Chris Corbold, SFX Supervisor

'We spent some time in Iceland testing the explosions on the trees. We wanted it to look like a spontaneous combustion, so tried a very soft way of igniting the trees, a very subtle use of pyrotechnics rather than just out and out destruction. The results were good. Oh, and we're not setting fire to the forest or destroying the environment – I think the trees are ex-Christmas trees that weren't sold.'
Chris Corbold, SFX Supervisor

Over page: Bond's Aston Martin V12 Vanquish

'I know we've seen cars on ice before but never like this, not amongst icebergs, giant ones forty, fifty feet high, sometimes several hundred yards across and tunnels of ice, quite astonishing. The ice was only about eight inches thick and that was a bit perilous. Everyone thought it wasn't going to work because we couldn't actually drive anything on ice. As it turned out we were blessed with just an unusually low temperature that froze the ice just enough.'
Lee Tamahori, Director

'When I saw dailies after shooting, I felt like we had discovered the new monument valley. The thing about this is that no one will probably be able to shoot here again because this ice is going to melt, this is the coldest winter in sixty-five years. So the chances of anyone else getting what we've got is very minimal.'
Vic Armstrong, Second Unit Director

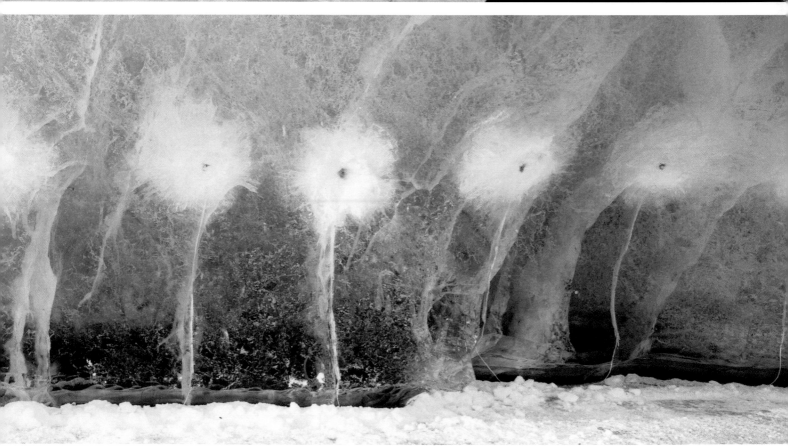

'We all know that stuntmen have a healthy appetite for mechanical equipment. So they are not too worried about smashing up the vehicles, we've made four Astons and four Jags. We know we are going to roll two of the Astons so if we then get a mechanical problem we still have another car available. If the stuntmen have done their job properly and we've done ours, there should be none left. The cars should be done to death and the film looks great!'
Andy Smith, Workshop Supervisor

Above: Jinx being tortured by Zao
on a diamond-cutting machine

An elaborate stunt involving Zao's Jaguar crashing through the Ice Palace

Above: Director Lee Tamahori with
Vic Armstrong, Second Unit Director
Left: Mr Kil played by Lawrence Makoare

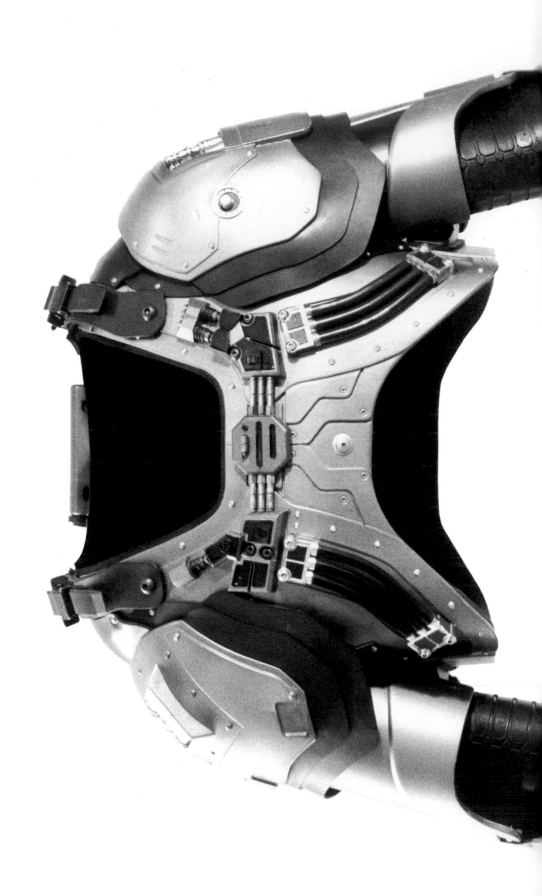

The Brassard Suit. The arm
control concentrates the sun's
rays onto targets on earth

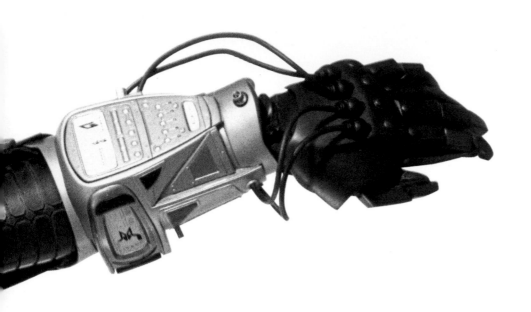

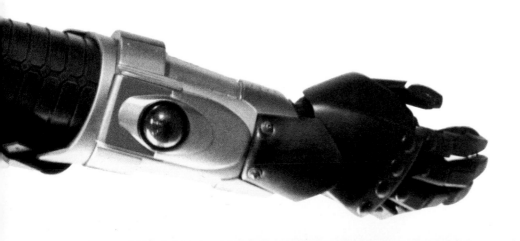

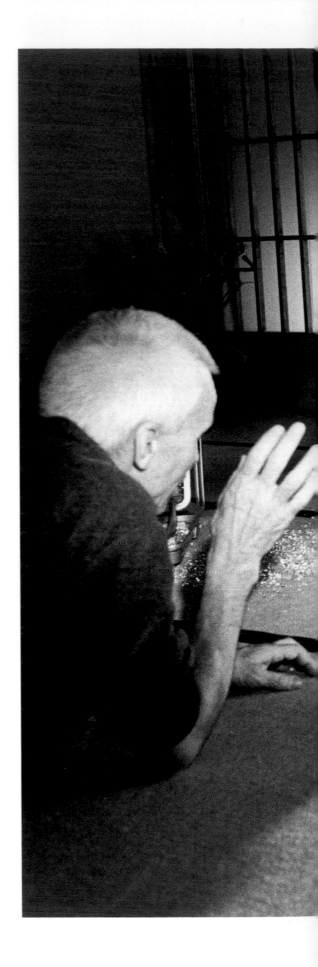

'It's very hard to sum up in a few words but Bond is this guy who all the guys want to be like – it's this fantasy character. You know it's the women, the sex, the cars and the gadgets. The ultimate hero.'
Pierce Brosnan, 007

145

REHEARSAL
ENTER QUIETLY

SHOOTING
NO ENTRY

ACKNOWLEDGEMENTS
GREG WILLIAMS

Thank you to the producers, Michael Wilson and Barbara Broccoli, for allowing me such exceptional access. And to all the cast, crew and everyone behind the scenes at EON and Pinewood who enabled me to work so freely and made me feel so welcome. Additional thanks to Pierce Brosnan for his introduction.

I cannot thank Anne Bennett enough for giving me this dream job. This project would have been impossible without the relentless hard work and support from her and the whole marketing and publicity team at EON.

Huge thanks to Mike Bone at Bostock and Pollitt for the book design and his passion for all things Bond.

At Boxtree, thanks to Gordon Wise, Emma Marriot, Natalie Jerome and Chris Gibson and at Midas PR, Emma Draude.

Thank you to Derek Francis at Metro and the printers Kathy Dixon [black and white] and Phill Keeble [colour].

To everyone at my agency, Growbag, especially Gareth Woods-Jack and Chris Ellis.

And finally, thank you to my sweetheart Sarah, Mum and Dad, Olly, Lisa and Bear and all my close friends for their love and support.

Greg started his career as a photojournalist working on foreign news assignments and in depth medical features. For the past five years he has worked largely within the entertainment industry as a special access freelance reportage and portrait photographer.

His first book *Greg Williams – On Set* was published in 2000.

His photos made with the artists Olly and Suzi will form part of a major book of their work to be published in 2003.

His photos have been exhibited widely and appeared in many of the worlds leading publications including *The Sunday Times Magazine*, *Stern* and *Vanity Fair*.

CAST

James Bond	Pierce Brosnan
Jinx	Halle Berry
Gustav Graves	Toby Stephens
Miranda Frost	Rosamund Pike
Zao	Rick Yune
M	Judi Dench
Q	John Cleese
Falco	Michael Madsen
Colonel Moon	Will Yun Lee
General Moon	Kenneth Tsang
Raoul	Emilio Echevarria
Vlad	Michael Gorevoy
Mr Kil	Lawrence Makoare
Robinson	Colin Salmon
Moneypenny	Samantha Bond
Snooty Desk Clerk	Ben Wee
Hotel Manager	Ho Yi
Peaceful	Rachel Grant
Creep	Ian Pirie
Dr Alvarez	Simon Andreu
Van Bierk	Mark Dymond
Air Hostess	Deborah Moore
Concierge 'Blades' Club	Oliver Skeete
Old man in Cigar Factory	Joaquin Martinez
General Chandler	Michael G. Wilson
General Han	Daryl Kwan
General Li	Vincent Wong
General Dong	Stuart Ong
Cuban Waiter	Manolo Caro
Korean Scorpion Guard	Tymarah
Doctor	Paul Darrow
Medic	Lucas Hare
Nurse	Cristina Contes
Reporter 1	Stewart Scudamore
Reporter 2	Bill Nash
Reporter 3	James Wallace
Reporter 4	Ami Chorlton

CREW

Michael G. Wilson	Producer
Barbara Broccoli	Producer
Lee Tamahori	Director
Neal Purvis	Writer
Robert Wade	Writer
Anthony Waye	Executive Producer
Callum McDougall	Co-Producer
Peter Lamont	Production Designer
David Tattersall BSC	Director Of Photography/1st Unit
Christian Wagner	Editor
Lindy Hemming	Costume Designer
David Arnold	Composer
Vic Armstrong	2nd Unit Director
George Aguilar	Stunt Coordinator
Chris Corbould	Special Effects Supervisor
Debbie McWilliams	Casting Director
John Richardson	Model Unit Supervisor
Mara Bryan	Visual Effects Supervisor
Danny Kleinman	Main Title Designer
Gerry Gavigan	1st Assistant Director/1st Unit
Peter Robertson	Camera Operator
Chris Munro	Sound Mixer
Anna Worley	Script Supervisor
Simon Lamont	Supervising Art Director
Simon Wakefield	Set Decorator
Ty Teiger	Property Master
Paul Hayes	Construction Manager
Martin Asbury	Storyboard Film Stylist
Bob Anderson	Sword Master
Steve Hamilton	SFX Floor Supervisor/1st Unit
Peter Notley	SFX Floor Supervisor/2nd Unit
Roy Quinn	Workshop Supervisor
Paul Knowles	Workshop Supervisor
Nick Finlayson	Workshop Supervisor
Andy Smith	Workshop Supervisor
Eddie Knight	Gaffer
Stewart Monteith	Best Boy
Colin Jamison	Hair Supervisor
Paul Engelen	Make-up Supervisor
Rick Provenzano	Hairdresser To Mr Brosnan
Bron Roylance	Make-up Artist To Mr Brosnan
Sterfon Demings	Hairdresser To Ms Berry
Mary Burton	Make-up Artist To Ms Berry
Simon Marsden	Location Manager
Philip Kohler	Location Manager
Anne Bennett	Director Of Marketing
Geoff Freeman	Unit Publicist/1st Unit
Geraldine Maloney	Unit Publicist/2nd Unit
Keith Hamshere	1st Unit Stills Photographer
Jay Maidment	2nd Unit Stills Photographer
Terry Madden	1st Assistant Director/2nd Unit
Jonathan Taylor	Director Of Photography/2nd Unit
Peter Field	Camera Operator/2nd Unit
Sharon Mansfield	Script Supervisor/2nd Unit

Publisher's note: During the seven months of production over one thousand people worked on *Die Another Day* and we regret that, due to lack of space, we are unable to list the names of all the actors and crew who participated in the making of the film.

JAMES BOND WILL RETURN